ORIOLES

BACKYARD BIRDS

Lynn Stone

The Rourke Corporation, Inc.
Vero Beach, Florida 32964

© 1998 The Rourke Corporation, Inc.

PHOTO CREDITS
© Tom Vezo: cover, pages 4, 7, 12, 13, 17, 21; © Lynn M. Stone: pages 10, 18, title page; © Tom Ulrich: page 8; page 15 courtesy Perky-Pet Products Company, Denver, CO

COVER ART:
James Spence

EDITORIAL SERVICES:
Penworthy Learning Systems

Library of Congress Cataloging-in-Publication Data

Stone, Lynn M.
   Orioles / by Lynn M. Stone.
     p. cm. — (Backyard birds)
   Includes index
   Summary: Describes the physical characteristics, habitats, and behavior of various kinds of these backyard birds including the northern and orchard orioles.
   ISBN 0-86593-474-6
   1. Icterus (Birds)—Juvenile literature. [1. Orioles.] I. Title II. Series. Stone, Lynn M. Backyard birds.
QL696.P2475S76 1998
598.8'74—dc21   98–2726
                                                           CIP
                                                           AC

Printed in the USA

TABLE OF CONTENTS

ORIOLES

The northern oriole is one of America's most loved backyard birds. The male's dazzling black and orange feathers always turn heads. The northern oriole's voice is beautiful, too. The oriole calls with a clear whistle, like a flute.

The northern oriole was once known as the Baltimore oriole. It is the state bird of Maryland, home of the city of Baltimore.

The northern oriole likes treetops near forest edges. Its cousin, the orchard oriole, lives in open places around towns, farms, and orchards.

The Baltimore variety of northern oriole is the state bird of Maryland.

WHAT ORIOLES LOOK LIKE

Orioles are medium-sized **perching** (PERCH ing) birds. The size depends upon the **species** (SPEE sheez), or kind, of oriole.

The northern oriole is about 7 inches (18 centimeters) long, about as long as a cardinal. The orchard oriole is about 6 inches (15 centimeters) long.

All male orioles of North America look much the same. Their breasts, bellies, and rumps have bright colors. Their wings, heads, and throats are black.

Female orioles are dull yellow. Each kind of female oriole is hard to tell from another.

The orchard oriole is darker than the northern oriole and prefers farmland to forest.

WHERE ORIOLES LIVE

The northern and orchard orioles have huge ranges, or living areas. The northern oriole lives across the United States and in much of southern Canada. The orchard oriole lives all over the United States east of the Rocky Mountains.

The Scott's oriole and the hooded oriole live in the Southwest. Three other species of orioles, normally found only in Mexico, sometimes visit the southwest U.S.

The Scott's oriole lives in Mexico and the southwest.

THE ORIOLE FAMILY

Eight species of orioles live in the United States at least part-time. Ten more species, almost never found in the United States, live in Mexico.

Orioles are the flashy members of their family, which includes meadowlarks and blackbirds. All members of the blackbird-oriole group have some black feathers. Most of these birds have some orange or yellow feathers, too.

The oriole family has some skilled singers. Two of the best are the orchard oriole and the meadowlark.

The yellow-headed blackbird is a cousin of the orioles.

The Bullock's variety of the northern oriole lives in the West.

A female Baltimore oriole feeds on an orange in a backyard in New York.

ORIOLES IN THE BACKYARD

Orioles are not seen often at winter **feeding stations** (FEE ding STAY shunz), or birdfeeders. Most orioles leave the United States by October. They spend winter south of the U.S. border, in Mexico.

During warm months orioles do sometimes visit feeders. They also visit backyards for things to build nests. You can leave pieces of string, wood shavings, cotton yarn, and strips of cloth for orioles.

Orioles in summer like feeders filled with sugar water.

BACKYARD FOOD FOR ORIOLES

The northern orioles that visit feeders like berries, orange slices, **suet** (SOO it), and nutmeats. Both the northern and hooded orioles also like syrup. Sometimes orioles use hummingbird feeders to sip sugar water. Orchard orioles will try jelly on bread.

Many natural foods attract orioles. They like the seeds of hollyhocks and sunflowers. Orioles also like pears, cherries, and the **nectar** (NEK tur) of trumpet vine. Nectar is sweet liquid made by some plants.

An orchard oriole in Texas visits a backyard feeder for a taste of sugar water.

ORIOLE HABITS

Some birds are **residents** (REZ eh dents) of a place. Resident birds live in the same area all year. Orioles, though, like robins, red-winged blackbirds, and many other birds, spend winter in warm places. They are called **migrants** (MY grunts), because they migrate, or travel long distances.

Orchard orioles begin their journey from north to south in July and August. That time is very early for migrants to travel. Northern orioles migrate south in September and October.

Hooded orioles of the Southwest migrate into Mexico each fall.

ORIOLE NESTS

The pioneers of early America called the northern oriole "fiery hang-nest." The male birds' bright orange looks like fire. Northern oriole nests do hang like little bags. When the wind blows, the northern oriole's nest swings gently.

The altimara oriole's nest hangs, too, like a stocking of grass. The hooded oriole's nest is a little basket made of grass.

Altimara oriole looks out of its hanging nest.

ORIOLE BABIES

The two most common American orioles, the northern and orchard, raise their babies in much the same way.

A mother oriole usually lays four or five eggs. She sits on her eggs, or **incubates** (IN kyuh BAYTS), to keep them warm. After about two weeks of mother's warmth, the eggs hatch.

Baby orioles grow up on insects brought to them by their parents. The young birds, called **nestlings** (NEST lingz), grow quickly. They can fly when two weeks old.

Glossary

feeding station (FEE ding STAY shun) — a place where people put food for birds; a birdfeeder

incubate (IN kyuh BAYT) — to keep eggs warm until they hatch

migrant (MY grunt) — an animal that migrates, or travels, long distances at the same time each year

nectar (NEK tur) — a sugary liquid made by some flowers; an important food for some birds and insects

nestling (NEST ling) — a young bird still in the nest and needing its parents to provide food

perching (PERCH ing) — any of the smaller birds, such as orioles, whose feet allow them to land on branches or other perches

resident (REZ eh dent) — an animal that remains within one home area throughout the year

species (SPEE sheez) — within a group of closely related animals, one certain kind, such as a *northern* oriole

suet (SOO it) — hardened animal fat

INDEX

FURTHER READING:

Find out more about Backyard Birds with these helpful books and information sites:
- Burnie, David. *Bird*. Knopf, 1988
- Cooper, Jason. *Birds, the Rourke Guide to State Symbols*. Rourke, 1997
- Mahnken, Jan. *The Backyard Bird-Lover's Guide.* Storey Communications, 1996
- Parsons, Alexandra. *Amazing Birds*. Knopf, 1990
- *Field Guide to the Birds of North America*. National Geographic, 1983
- Cornell Laboratory of Ornithology online at http://birdsource.cornell.edu
- National Audubon Society online at www.audubon.org